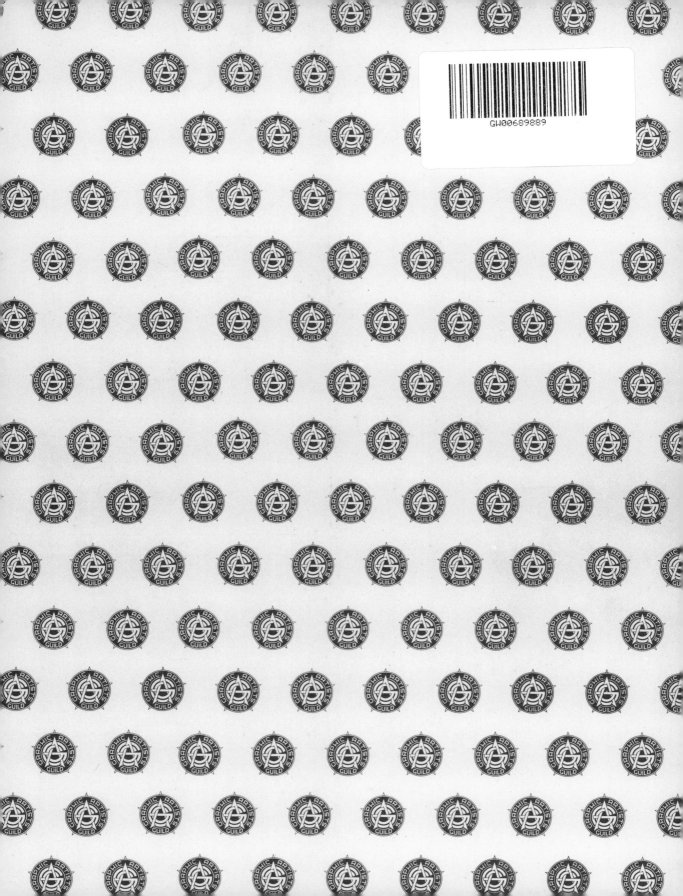

Graphic Artists Guild's
Corporate & Communications
Design Annual

ANNUALS PUBLISHING CO.

CORPORATE & COMMUNICATIONS
DESIGN ANNUAL

Copyright © Graphic Artists Guild, Inc. 1984
All Rights Reserved
The design contained in this publication is
protected by copyright in the name of the
designer. No design in this publication may
be reproduced in any form without obtaining
permission from the designer.
Distributors to the trade in the United States:
Contemporary Books, Inc., 180 North
Michigan Avenue, Chicago, IL 60601
Distributed in Continental Europe by:
Feffer and Simons, B.V. 170 Rijnkade,
    Weesp, Netherlands
Distributed throughout the rest of the world by:
Fleetbooks, S.A. % Feffer and Simons, Inc.,
    100 Park Avenue, New York, NY 10017
ISBN 0-912417-02-1
Annuals Publishing Company, Inc.,
    10 East 23rd Street, New York,
    NY 10010   (212) 475-1620
Distributor to the art-supply trade:
Robert Silver Associates, 95 Madison
    Avenue, New York, NY 10010

ANNUALS PUBLISHING COMPANY, INC.

Publishers *Arie Kopelman, Gerald
    McConnell, Tad Crawford*
Marketing Director *Pauline Augustine*
Art Director *Warren Rogers*
Production Manager *Cathy Citarella*
Production Assistant *Ellise Fuchs*
Comptroller *Jonathan Greenbaum*
Distribution Director *Kristin Crawford*
Traffic Manager *Katherine Brown*
Administrative Assistant *Zulema Rodriguez*
Book Design *Walter Bernard*
Graphic Artists Guild Logo *Michael Doret*
Typography *Advani Typographic Assoc.*
Printed in Japan by Dai Nippon

*We wish to thank the
Advisory Board of Directory 4
and Corporate & Communications
Design Annual*

Co-Chairperson
RACQUEL BALIN
Illustrator/Graphic Designer

LLYNE BUSCHMAN
Illustrator/Graphic Designer

MICHAEL GARLAND
Illustrator

Co-Chairperson
EVELYNE JOHNSON
Artist's Representative

JOHN KNEAPLER
Corporate & Package Designer

DON LEAKE
Illustrator

ROBERT RODRIGUEZ
Illustrator

Project Coordinator
D.K. HOLLAND
*Executive Vice President
Graphic Artists Guild National*

TIBOR KALMAN
Graphic Designer

SEYMOUR CHWAST
Graphic Designer

BRENT MARMO
Graphic Designer

JOHN WATERS
Graphic Designer

Table of Contents

NATIONAL BOARD
OF DIRECTORS

Chairman
REGINA ORTENZI
President
JEFF SEAVER
Vice President
SIMMS TABACK
Vice President
GERALD McCONNELL
Secretary
JAN GIOLITO
Assistant Secretary
BOB RUSSO
Treasurer
GALE LITVAK
Assistant Treasurer
DARLENE FEINEN

FOUNDATION OFFICERS

President
SIMMS TABACK
Vice President
ELIZABETH COOK
Treasurer
JEFF SEAVER

GRAPHIC ARTISTS
GUILD STATEMENT

With the explosion of new technologies and information systems in the past several years, graphic design firms have burgeoned as major visual image makers for society's messages. Graphic designers have become an integral part of the Graphic Artists Guild, bringing with them a rich artistic tradition, new slants on issues the Guild has been active in such as: standard contracts and business terms, pricing structures and ethical business practices. They have also added new energies and commitments to Guild activities.

Publishers Statement

*T*his volume arose out of the needs of both leading design professionals and the corporations they work with.

It is a tool for both presenting and evaluating the wide latitude of approaches available in all phases of design, marketing and corporate communications.

Our intention is to provide corporate managers with greater access to design resources, and design firms with enhanced opportunity for individual recognition.

The Publishers

"Design is a process in which needs or wants represent the problem, while ideas represent possible solutions."

George Nelson

GOTTSCHALK + ASH INTERNATIONAL
Design Consultants

170 Fifth Avenue
New York, New York 10010
(212) 807-0011

*D*ESIGN IS COMMUNICATION. Good design has the power to involve, inform, motivate and sell. It translates emotion into images and creates lasting impressions. How your organization is perceived by all of its audiences depends greatly on the effectiveness of your design program.

Gottschalk + Ash International believes that design must reflect the best basic qualities of each client's organization, product or personality. It must speak to the client's public directly and clearly, yet with great imagination to attract and hold attention.

American Stock Exchange:
Corporate Identity Program

IBM:
Promotional Poster

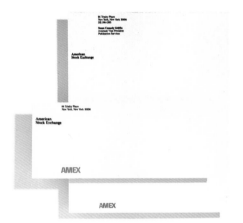

Identity Programs and
Systems Development

Corporate Identity
Corporate Identity Manuals
Publication Programs

Special Events
Promotions

Posters
Conference Materials
Sales Material
Recognition Events

Gottschalk + Ash International offers a comprehensive service from project analysis and preliminary design concepts through production and printing. Schedule and budget requirements are adhered to while producing high quality results which meet corporate objectives. This project management, attention to detail, and commitment to design excellence has resulted in satisfied clients and a body of work which has been recognized and awarded for outstanding achievement.

For further information contact:
Kenneth Carbone, Principal
Leslie Smolan, Principal

Current Client List:
Morgan Guaranty Trust Company
Merrill Lynch
Citicorp
Swiss Bank Corporation
Chase Manhattan Bank
American Stock Exchange
GTE Corporation
Museum of Modern Art

GTE:
Annual Report

Citibank:
Computer Manual

External Corporate
Communications

Annual Reports
Quarterly Reports
Capability Brochures
Recruiting Brochures

Internal Corporate
Communications

Training and Benefits Manuals
Employee Publications
Newsletters
Corporate Magazines

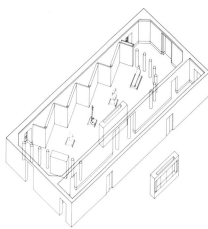

Exhibition:
AIA SF 100; centennial
exhibition for the S.F.
Chapter of the American
Institute of Architects,
at the San Francisco
Museum of Modern Art.

Poster:
The Stanford Confer-
ence on Design Poster;
Stanford Alumni Associ-
ation, client.

Brochure:
Cover and typical
spreads from a capability
brochure for an architec-
tural firm; Anshen and
Allen, client.

Brochure:
The Executive Guide to
Office Planning; Eugene Lew
and Associates, client.

Symbol:
Century City
Shopping Center
in Los Angeles.

Symbol:
Eastface, ski con-
dominiums on the
eastern slope of the
Sierra Nevadas;
Robert Ostrow,
client.

HUNT, SNODGRASS, INCORPORATED

3312 Piedmont Road
Suite 530
Atlanta, Georgia 30305
(404) 231-2060

*H*UNT, SNODGRASS SPECIALIZES in the development of printed communications for business. Headed by Rhoda Hunt and Charles Snodgrass, the firm takes a problem-solving approach to communications design, with strong emphasis on the qualities of corporate visual image. And they provide a totally-managed package of creative and production services, from concept through printing.

Hunt, Snodgrass has developed communications for such firms as:
CNN Radio/Turner Broadcasting
The Belton Corporation

The Candler Building
*Elson's
*Equifax, Inc.
*Georgia Footwear, Inc.
 A.W. Hutchison & Associates
*IBM
 ML&M Services, Inc.
 William M. Mercer, Inc.
 ONE Corporation

The Parkland Corporation
Peachtree Center
Peachtree Software, Inc./MSA
RFD Enterprises
*Royal Crown Companies, Inc.
 Scalamandre
*Southeastern Travelers Exhibitors
*Spectronics, Inc.
 Spirit Homes, Inc.

J.M. Tull Industries, Inc.
*Arthur Young & Company

(*)Illustrated below

PHOTOGRAPHY BY TIM GUERRY,
ATLANTA/CHICAGO

SEITZ YAMAMOTO MOSS INC.

252 First Avenue North
Minneapolis, MN 55401
(612) 375-0180

*C*ORPORATE IDENTITY SYSTEMS,
Annual Reports, Packaging, Sales
and Marketing brochures, Signage
and Exhibition design.

Clients include:
3M, Honeywell, Pillsbury, Control
Data, Deluxe Check Printers,
American Medical Systems, Data

Card, Wilson Learning, Inc., DEI,
Minnegasco, Northwestern and
National Life, Lutheran Brother-
hood, National Computer
Systems, Trane Sentinel, Peavey,
CPT, and Target.

Shown below:
SYM office interiors; Pillsbury
Annual Report cover, Appletree
Square Capabilities brochure,
Peavey Annual Report cover and
inside spread.

M&Co.

157 West 57th Street
New York, NY 10019
(212) 582-7050

M&Co. founded: 1979
Full-time employees: 6
Contact:
Tibor Kalman, President

Clients:
ABC Leisure
ABC Publishing
American Express Bank
Barnes&Noble
Bloomingdale's
Carnegie Hall
Duggal Color Projects
Geer, DuBois
Harvard Lampoon
IBM
Island Records
J.P. Stevens
Lincoln Center
Manufacturers Hanover
Marshall Field's
National Lampoon
Ogilvy & Mather
Remy Martin
Revlon
R.J. Reynolds
Warner Bros Records
Warner Communications

Areas of
particular interest:
Promotional Marketing
Youth Marketing
Publication Development
and Design
Electronic Graphics
Film & Video Titles

MAKE IT "SM

—MANUFACTURE

"DIGNIFIED"

—FACTS ON FILE, INC.

"ELEGANT"

—NATIONAL AUDUBON SOCIETY

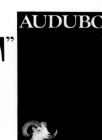

"HOT"

—HANNIBAL RECORDS

"SE

—TENBA, I

"SING"

—CARNEGIE HALL

ART"  "FUNNY"

NOVER TRUST

—THE HARVARD LAMPOON

 "INNOVATIVE"

—WARNER BROS. RECORDS

SNAPPY"  "COOL"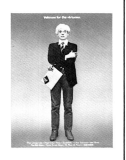

—CRUSHING ENTERPRISES, INC.

—STAT STORE, INC.

 "SWEET"

—M&Co.

MAKE IT  M&Co.

PIRTLE DESIGN

4528 McKinney
Suite 104
Dallas, Texas 75205
(214) 522-7520

*D*ESIGN SERVICES RANGING
from corporate identity programs
and annual reports to packaging
and point of purchase materials.

The following is a partial listing of
past and present clients.
American Airlines
Cadillac Fairview
Celanese Corporation
Centex Corporation
Cincinnati Symphony
Dallas Museum of Art
Dallas Opera
Dallas Symphony
Diamond Shamrock Corporation
Fabergé
Harte-Hanks Communications
    Corporation
Gerald D. Hines Interests
JMB/Federated Realty
    Assoc., Ltd.
Knoll International
National Gypsum Company
Neiman-Marcus
The Rouse Company
Simpson Paper Company
Southland Corporation
Sports Illustrated
Texas Instruments
Towers, Perrin, Forster & Crosby
T.G.I. Friday's, Incorporated
Urban Investment & Development
    Company

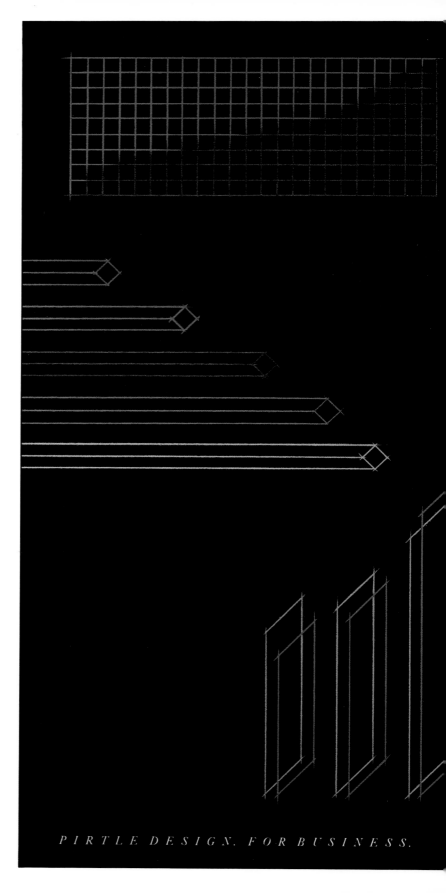

PIRTLE DESIGN. FOR BUSINESS.

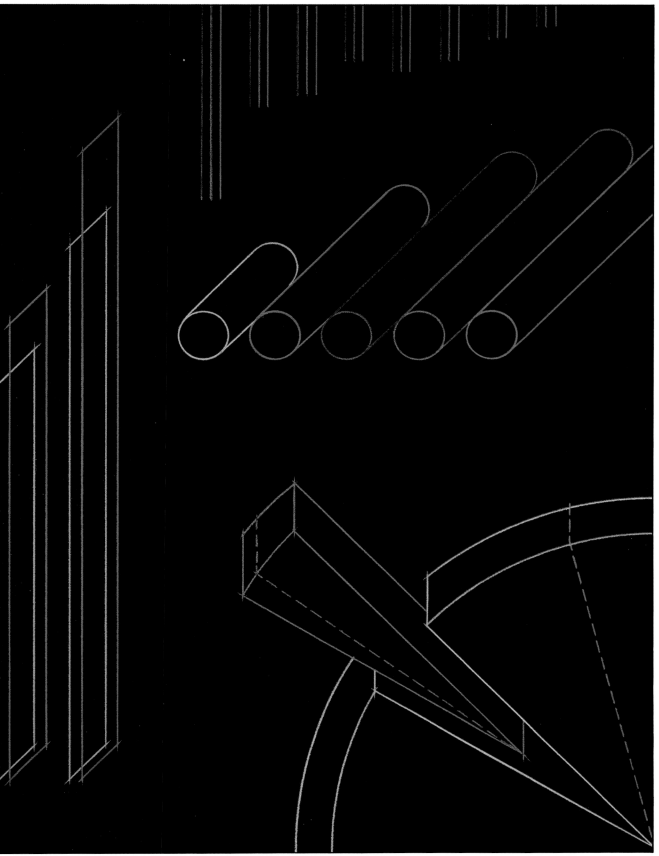

21

JOHN WATERS ASSOCIATES, INC.

3 West 18th Street
New York, New York 10011
(212) 807-0717

*I*dentity Design:
Visual Audits
Image Analysis
Identity Systems
Trademarks

Communications Design:
Literature Systems
Annual Reports
Advertising
Sales Promotion

Environmental Design:
Architectural Graphics
Exhibits
Interiors
Signage

Clients:
Arab Bank Limited
Arrow Electronics, Inc.
Curtiss-Wright Corporation
Drexel Burnham Lambert
Dworkin Construction
Florida Capital Corporation
General Signal Corporation
Gilman Paper Company
The Gunlocke Company
Jones Lang Wooton
Mutual of New York
National Distillers
New York University
RBS&D Architects, Inc.
Smith Barney, Inc.
Sony Corporation
Turner Construction Company
UBAF Arab American Bank

HILL/A GRAPHIC DESIGN GROUP

2626 Westheimer, Suite 200
Houston, Texas 77098
(713) 523-7363

*H*ILL, A GRAPHIC DESIGN GROUP, specializes in the development of marketing programs for a variety of commercial and institutional clients. Their designs include corporate identities, annual reports, collateral materials, advertising campaigns and total marketing communications.

Chris Hill, principal of the group directs the firm's creative output. He and his studio are recognized as a firm that produces award-winning designs and solid solutions to their client's marketing problems.

Hill has prepared a sample portfolio.

It is available upon request.

Partial Client List:
Alfa Acero, Monterrey, Mexico
The Art Directors Club
  of New York
James Avery Craftsman
Big Brothers/Big Sisters
Boy Scouts of America
Champion Realty Corporation
City of Corpus Christi

Conoco Oil
Fairmont Hotels
The Farb Companies
Fidelity Capital Corporation
Galveston-Houston Company
Gerald D. Hines Interests
Harvey Construction Company
Horizon Mortgage Corporation
Houston Grand Opera

Houston Museum of Fine Arts
Houstonian Development
The M.W. Kellogg Company
NCAA
The Rouse Company
Software Express
Tampa, Florida, Int'l. Airport
Texas Investment Bank
Zebec Data Systems, Inc.

THE BROWNSTONE GROUP, INC.

27A St. Mary's Court
Brookline, MA 02146

Represented by Lisa Bassett
(617) 566-7330

*T*O THE BROWNSTONE GROUP, INC., design is problem solving. Each client and each client's project demands individual focus, keeping in mind corporate image, product image, the marketplace, function, schedule, and budget. Responding to this general project criteria and to the levels of information needed to be communicated, The Brownstone Group provides design, production, and management of each project through to a unique and comprehensive solution.

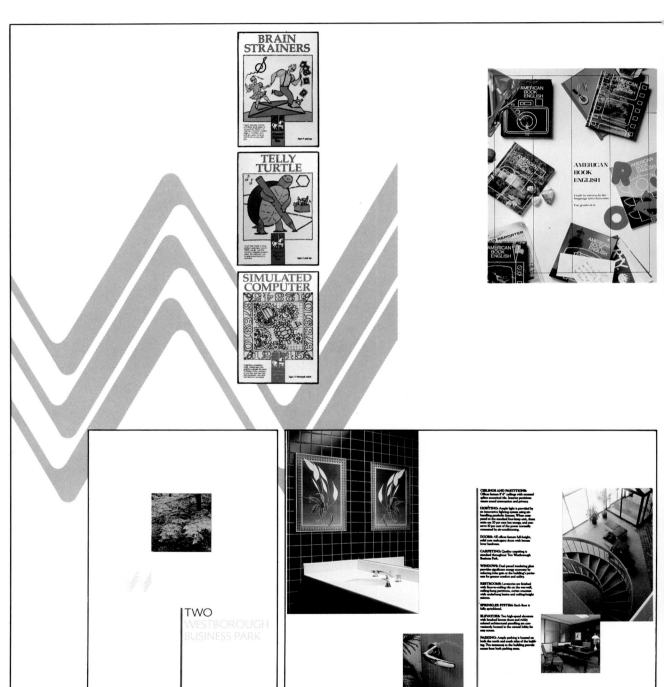

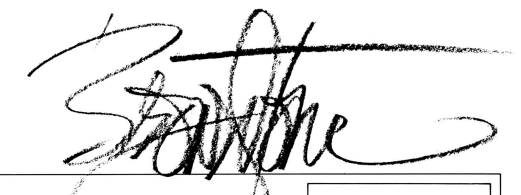

Hands-on activities introduce children in kinder-garten and grade 1 to the language arts as they match colors and numbers with their names.

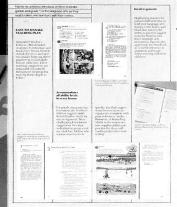

EASY-TO-MANAGE TEACHING PLAN

Involves parents

Accommodates all ability levels in every lesson

PROJECT
プロジェクト
projectos
Projets
計劃
PROJECTOS

P R O J E C T S

プロジェクト

PROJECT CASE STUDY

Kyoto's Life-Giving Network

In the modern hospital many important decisions are dependent on the speed and accuracy of communicating vital information.

At the Kyoto University Hospital in Japan, the entire staff is involved in an innovative sharing of resources using a Digital standard HL7/MPS computer network system.

The result is quality health care, with the added benefit of smooth administrative operations.

Software Services

CALL FOR ACTION

Software Services

TELEPHONE SUPPORT

SOFTWARE PRODUCT SERVICE

SOFTWARE SERVICES

PROJECTS

PROJECT CASE STUDY

Amatil's Decision

Amatil is Australia's most diversified international manufacturing corporation in the food, tobacco, print-ing, and packaging industries. Its subsidiary companies make autonomous decisions about what computer services to use.

The Management Services Department (MSD) of Amatil, which runs a Computer Resource Centre, was challenged to supply a system that could compete with outside soft-ware service bureaus and computer vendors to provide the best solutions to the computer needs of Amatil's subsid-iaries. They did an extensive analysis of vendors. Digital's investment in research and development, and proven track record convinced Amatil that Digital had the range of prod-ucts and services to meet the needs of a large organization and could best increase their prospects for the future.

JONSON PEDERSEN HINRICHS & SHAKERY, INC.

141 Lexington Avenue
New York, New York 10016
(212) 889-9611

*J*ONSON PEDERSEN HINRICHS & Shakery, Inc.'s work covers a broad range of design communications, from packaging and product design through corporate identification programs and communications.

A partial listing of clients includes:

AT&T Co.
American Airlines
American Express Co.
Atari Games
Bell Labs
Big River Mining
Business Week Magazine
CBS Publications
Champion International Corp.
Chevrolet
Dow Jones & Co., Inc.
Eastern Airlines
FAO Schwarz
Field & Stream
General Electric Co.
Hopper Paper (Georgia-Pacific
    Corp.)
Knoll International
Nautical Quarterly, Inc.
Puerto Rico Industrial Develop-
    ment Co.
Royal Viking Line
Sonnenblick-Goldman Corp.
Steelcase
Warner Communications, Inc.
Xerox Corporation.

NAUTICAL QUARTERLY

The Pierre

AMERICAN EXPRESS COMPANY ANNUAL REPORT

DOW JONES ANNUAL REPORT 1982

Sonnenblick-Goldman

489 PARK AVENUE

BusinessWeek

ILL PUBLICATION   SPECIAL REPORT   APRIL 25, 1983 ● $2.00

NEW ERA FOR MANAGEMENT

E SHRINKING OF MIDDLE MANAGEMENT
OMPUTER-RUN OFFICES AND FACTORIES
A DISENCHANTED MIDDLE CLASS
WHY INTEREST RATES STAY HIGH
ORATE STRATEGIES: TOSHIBA • PONDEROSA

STRANDELL DESIGN

233 East Wacker Drive, Suite 3609
Chicago, Illinois 60601
(312) 861-1654

*S*TRANDELL DESIGN WORK HAS
no one particular style. They feel
each client demands and deserves
a unique graphic approach. Therefore, Strandell does their best work
with clients who want to become
deeply involved with their projects . . . those who recognize
exceptional graphics as an important marketing tool.

STRANDELL DESIGN

Graphic Design Consultants

Specializing in identities for corporations, products, and services.

Recipients of many national awards.

Client: Park Hyatt
Project: Logotype and Identity Program

PARK HYATT.®

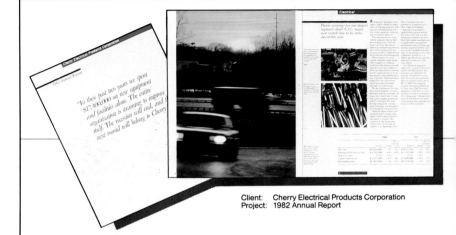

Client: Cherry Electrical Products Corporation
Project: 1982 Annual Report

Client: Windsor Court Hotel
Project: Logotype and Identity

WINDSOR COURT HOTEL

NEW ORLEANS

Designe

Client: Gingiss Formalwear
Project: Logotype and New Bag Design

Serengeti
eyewear

Client: Foote, Cone & Belding/Corning Glass
Project: Logotype

Client: Medical Directions/Abbott Laboratories
Project: Logotype for new corporate division

Client: Multivision International
Project: Logotype and Identity Program

**Abbott
HomeCare
Division**

MULTI

Client: Leo Burnett/Philip Morris
Project: Logotype and complete book design

Client: Della Femina Travisano & Partners/Permalens
Project: New Product Logotype

Permalens

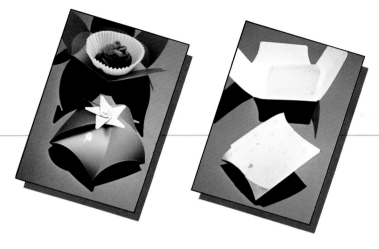

Client: Lee King/State of Illinois
Project: Logotype to promote Illinois tourism

Client: Park Hyatt
Project: Guest Amenities Packaging

Client: Kalamazoo College
Project: Recruitment Brochure

Client: Leo Burnett/Philip Morris
Project: Logotype for Women's Tennis Circuit

Client: A. G. Becker
Project: Product Identity

Client: Ram Tools
Project: Line of Package Designs

COOPER/COPELAND, INC.

1151 West Peachtree Street NW
Atlanta, Georgia 30309
(404) 892-3472

*B*RAD COPELAND AND DAVID
Cooper formed their studio to
pursue the notion that graphic design can depart from ordinary excellence. To achieve a consistent
level of conceptual distinction,
their studio specializes in corporate
projects that call for unique creative approaches.

Their design team has established
a reputation for individualized
service—providing a spectrum of
clients in communications, fashion,
home furnishings, and manufacturing with imagery that sets them
apart. Their talents apply with
equal facility to a wide range of design applications—from corporate

■ Corporate Advertising

■ Anniversary Edition Book

■ Commemorative Poster Design

■ Fashion Calendar

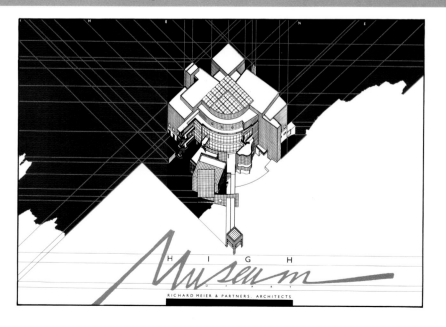

identity to advertising campaigns.

Clients include:
Turner Broadcasting Systems, Inc.
VideoStar Connections, Inc.
The Wine Spectrum
Atlanta Market Center
Habersham Plantation
Coca Cola

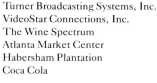

Corporate Profile Brochures

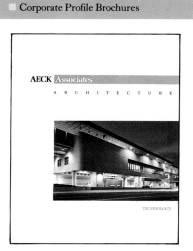

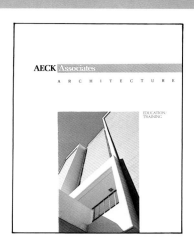

Design Exhibition Poster

Point of Purchase

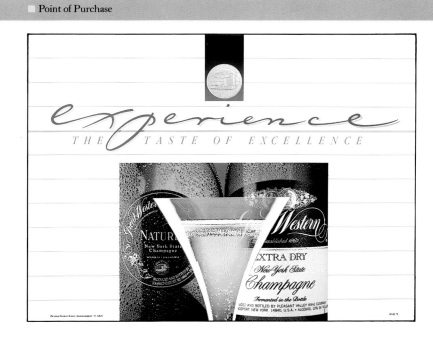

ROBERT ANTHONY INC.

10 East 23rd Street
New York, NY 10010
(212) 673-3011

WINNER OF MANY ACCOLADES within the graphic design field, Robert Anthony Inc. is a firm which has always based its design solutions on a thorough understanding of the client's problems. Its president, Robert Anthony, formerly with McCann Erickson and Norman, Craig & Kummel, brings a broad sales-promotion and marketing background to the firm he founded in 1967.

Corporate publications and I.D. programs, book designs, and promotional and merchandising projects are all carefully tailored to meet specific needs. In areas as varied as finance, real estate, restaurant/hotel, publishing, and architecture, this work has received awards from AIGA Communications Graphics, AIGA Cover Show, Art Directors Club, Type Directors Club, Creativity Print Case Books, Society of Illustrators and others.

Samples at right show but a few of the firm's diverse capabilities. For example, the E.F. Hutton promotion relating to AT&T included designing both client and broker material plus a vehicle to contain them. Among the Merrill Lynch projects: a major series of training aids including a nine-volume series, and annual reviews. Other current clients include Damson Oil, Lehman College, Simon & Schuster, Knopf, Houghton Mifflin, Holt, Rinehart & Winston and WETA (PBS).

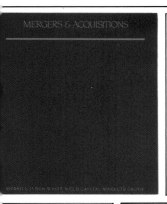

Merrill Lynch White Weld provides a broad range of services to assist our clients in conceiving, defining and executing their merger and acquisition objectives. Our Firm consistently ranks among the leading merger specialists on Wall Street — in both the number and the dollar value of transactions completed. Since 1978, when Merrill Lynch acquired White Weld, we have closed over 140 transactions with an aggregate value exceeding $21 billion. Over 50 of these corporate combinations had values in excess of $100 million. In addition, we have rendered extensive services in merger and acquisition assignments that remain confidential, such as performing valuations for domestic and foreign corporations, undertaking advance defensive preparation against unfriendly tender offers and performing strategic consulting work. Because of our continuous involvement in the merger marketplace, we are in a strong position to advise clients on achievable goals when they are considering mergers and acquisitions.

Within Merrill Lynch White Weld, the Mergers and Acquisitions Department is the center for professional services that relate to the acquisition or sale of a company or subsidiary, defensive preparedness, leveraged buyouts and financial advisory assignments. The extensive resources of Merrill Lynch provide the Department with the best merger-related information system in the world. The Department is a focal point for information received from the Firm's acclaimed Securities Research Division, from Merrill Lynch's global corporate and institutional contacts and from the largest equity trading and arbitrage departments on Wall Street. Our technological resources include sophisticated computer-based information storage and data-processing systems, which we use extensively to design valuation models and to simulate the potential financial effects of corporate combinations.

The professionals involved on each assignment work closely with our client's senior management throughout each step of the transaction process. A team typically includes one or more senior bankers from the Mergers and Acquisitions Department, junior staff members and, often, a generalist investment banker with particular knowledge about the client's industry and business.

While every assignment is unique, we believe that valuation is at the heart of the merger process. Therefore, we put special emphasis on a thorough understanding of past results

ANNUAL REVIEW

Merrill Lynch White Weld Capital Markets Group

The Merrill Lynch White Weld Capital Markets Group leads in providing creative financing and advisory capabilities, market making and trading capacities, and other financial services to corporate, institutional, and government entities. Merrill Lynch White Weld Capital Markets Group is the name under which Merrill Lynch & Co., Inc. conducts its investment banking business.

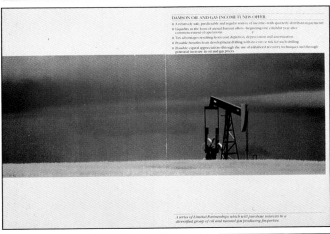

DAMSON OIL AND GAS INCOME FUNDS OFFER:

■ A relatively safe, predictable and regular source of income—with quarterly distribution payments
■ Liquidity in the form of annual buyout offers—beginning one calendar year after commencement of operations
■ Tax advantages resulting from cost depletion, depreciation and amortization
■ Possible benefits from development drilling with its cost or risk for such drilling
■ Possible capital appreciation—through the use of enhanced recovery techniques and through potential increase in oil and gas prices

A series of Limited Partnerships which will purchase interests in a diversified group of oil and natural gas producing properties.

EMERSON, WAJDOWICZ STUDIOS, INC.

1123 Broadway
New York, New York 10010
(212) 807-8144

European representative:
Geneva (22) 84-06-25

*Q*UALITY CAN MEAN DIFFERENT things. At Emerson, Wajdowicz Studios it means distinctive graphic design, typographical brilliance, technical expertise, clarity of vision. It means a unique approach to solving communications problems. It means cost-effectiveness. Ultimately, it means getting the client's message across—successfully. Quality is achieved in different ways. At Emerson, Wajdowicz it is achieved by a small, cohesive team working with highly efficient organization, a team whose members, starting with the partners, devote the kind of personal attention to the needs of the client or his agency

"HELLO, CENTRAL . . . PARK!"—Poster for New York Shakespeare Festival (New York Telephone, client)

THE EAST-WEST ROUND TABLE of New York—Symbol; part of visual identification program

THE EAST WEST ROUND TABLE OF NEW YORK

INNOCENTA—Logotype for fashion designer

"CHOOSING THE RIGHT TYPEFACES FOR YOUR WORK"—Type cover for corporate booklet for AM International (client)

that few more sprawling groups can manage. It is achieved through a sensitivity to those needs, through flexibility, through a very special blending of American and European training and values. Polish-born Jurek Wajdowicz directs the creative side of EWS. Before founding the Studio with Matt Emerson (who serves as European-American liaison from his base in Switzerland), he was Design Director for Design Processing International (DPI) and Art Director for Lubalin, Burns & Company. Quality is why Emerson, Wajdowicz has so quickly gained the reputation it has, both in the United States and in Europe, both in the design community and among clients. A few of those clients are: Alfred A. Knopf, Inc., Caran D'Ache (Lausanne, Switzerland), Dun & Bradstreet, Inc., Museum of Modern Art (Lodz, Poland), New York Telephone, and The New York Times Company.

718 and ACCESS CHARGES – Corporate capabilities brochures for New York Telephone (client)

VISION 80s – U&lc magazine (New York) and Charactère (Paris)

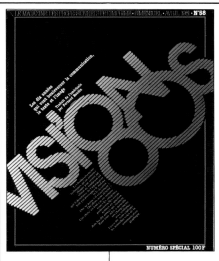

KANELBA & ROBILOTTI – Trademark; part of corporate identity program

"TAKE ANOTHER LOOK..." –Campaign logotype for New York Telephone (client)

RICHARDS, SULLIVAN, BROCK & ASSOCIATES

12700 Hillcrest Road, Suite 242
Dallas, Texas 75230
(214) 386-9077

Wᴇ'ᴠᴇ ᴅᴏɴᴇ ᴀɴ ᴀᴅ, ᴀɴ ᴀɴɴᴜᴀʟ report, a book jacket, a corporate book, a corporate identity program, an invitation, a logo, a matchbook, a packaging project, a poster, a radio spot, a TV commercial, and more award-winning work for clients from A to Z:

American Healthcare Management
Best Products Company
Business Week Magazine
Campbell Taggart, Inc.
Criswell Development Corporation
Dallas Times Herald
Datapoint Corporation
Denver Post
Federal Express Corporation
Frito-Lay
Harte-Hanks Communications
Holiday Inns, Inc.
Katy Railroad
Lincoln Hotel Corporation
Lomas & Nettleton
Mary Kay Cosmetics
Mercantile Texas Corporation
Newsweek Magazine
Northern Telecom Inc.
Overhead Door Corporation
Paragon Group, Inc.
G.P. Putnam Sons
The Rouse Company
The Southland Corp.
Sports Illustrated
Texas Instruments
Texas Monthly
Time Life Books
Time Magazine
Toms Foods
Tony Roma's Restaurants
Triton Energy Corporation
Vecta Contract, Inc.
The Dallas Zoo

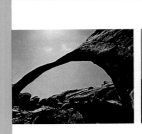

Lomas & Nettleton Financial Corporation / Annual Report

Lomas & Nettleton Mortgage Investors / Annual Report

Earth Grains Breads / Package Design

Texas Instruments / Product Promotion Poster

Hyatt Hotels

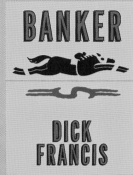

There isn't always room for improvement

Schroder Real Estate / Trade Ad

BANKER

DICK FRANCIS

G. P. Putnam Sons / Book Cover

SEASON'S READINGS.

Newsweek / Consumer Ad

Lincoln Hotels

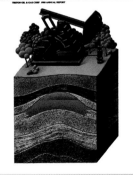

Triton Oil & Gas Corporation / Annual Report

The Summit at Crested Butte

Mercantile Texas Corporation / Annual Report

DALLAS ZOO

THE GNU GROUP

2200 Bridgeway Boulevard
Sausalito, California 94965
(415) 332-8010

*T*HE GNU GROUP IS A NATIONALLY recognized design firm providing services in three broadly based areas: image and identity programs, print communications, and environmental graphics.

"Design services represent an investment which should return a

profit to clients," explains Richard Burns, the firm's president. "End results are judged not only on the effectiveness of solutions but on the sound management of client budgets. Our creative process is predicated on market analyses and a business-oriented, logical approach to problem solving."

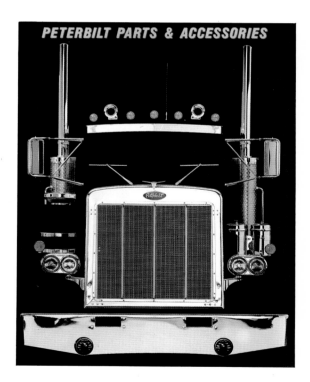

The glamour, image and quality associated with the Peterbilt name is translated in this catalog for the company's parts division.

Each issue of the Woodward-Clyde Consultants' corporate magazine explores in depth an area of the firm's capabilities.

The GNU Group accepts full responsibility for each project and provides comprehensive services from concept through production.

With offices in Sausalito, Houston, and Portland, The GNU Group works successfully with clients throughout the country.

A partial list of clients includes:

Abercrombie & Fitch Co.
California First Bank
Georgia Pacific
Gerald D. Hines Interests
Pacific Power & Light Company
Peterbilt Motor Company
Woodward-Clyde Consultants

Office locations:

602 Sawyer Street
Houston, Texas 77007
(713) 868-6086

2066 N.W. Irving
Portland, Oregon 97209
(503) 222-2266

California First Bank Annual Report 1981

California First Bank's annual report reflected a theme based upon a successful media campaign from the previous year.

The unique heritage as safari outfitters is reflected in this solution for Abercrombie&Fitch's packaging.

The logo for The Society of Environmental Graphics Designers visually expresses the function and purpose of the organization.

38 East 57 Street
New York, New York 10022
(212) 644-3850

*T*HE BEAUTY OF A DESIGN
lies in its ability
to influence an opinion,
convey a message
or stir an emotion.

Resource Manhattan
is a full-service creative group
currently working with some of
the most prestigious companies in
information technology, ballet,
banking and travel services,
cable television, publishing,
cosmetics, fragrance, fine china
and home furnishings textiles.

We can create or
transform your company's identity,
promote its services,
launch, package and display
its products.

Resource Manhattan offers
total creativity for business.

ROSS & HARVEY INCORPORATED

Graphic Design
500 N. Dearborn
Chicago, Il. 60610
(312) 467-1290

Ross & Harvey, Incorporated is engaged in all forms of graphic communications—providing concept and layout, as well as production and printing. Areas of expertise include identity programs, ad campaigns, point-of-purchase, packaging and collateral. The firm, which has been in existence for 8 years, is headed by award-winning designer/illustrators Marc Ross and Roger Harvey.

Client List:
McDonald's Corporation
Wilton Enterprises, Inc.
Wrigley-Amurol, Inc.
Food & Wine from France
Playboy, Inc.
United Airlines
Phillip Morris
James Joseph Cosmetics
Troy Thread & Textile Corp.
Hardee's Food Systems, Inc.
Mobil Oil Corp.

A. Package design for Guinness World Records card collection
B. Book on candy making
C. Mark and stationery for insurance underwriters
D. Spread from report by Continental X-Ray Corp.
E. Logo for Country & Western Awards
F. Package design and ad series for James Joseph Cosmetics
G. Symbols for Food & Wine from France
H. Logo for housing development
I. Logo for real estate company
J. Promotional package for retail franchise
K. Mark for computer softwear company
L. Logo for record company
M. Ad for LeCreuset Cookwear
N. Direct mail promotion for Sea-Pines resort
O. Theme design for ad campaign

C. **Lucky Dice.**

D. **Truffle Filled Ruffle and Rosy Rectangle.**

E. **Cordial Cherry.**

K

KRIYA

SWANK REAL ESTATE

Mexican Poppi

L

MAINSTREAM RECORDS

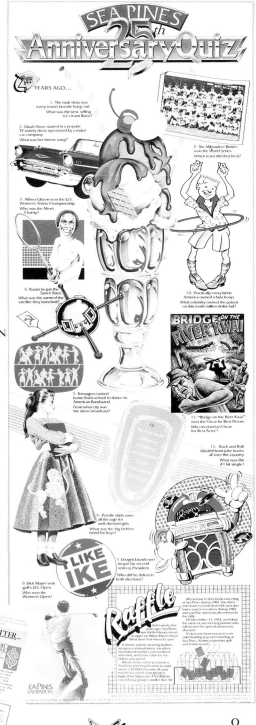

O

It's Magic!

PUSHPIN LUBALIN PECKOLICK, INC.

67 Irving Place
New York, NY 10003
(212) 674-8080

PUSHPIN LUBALIN PECKOLICK IS AN international graphic design office whose scope of work encompasses logos, corporate identity, annual reports, magazine and book design, posters, packaging, TV animation, exhibition, industrial, environmental design and implementation. The company serves clients world- wide through its affiliate in England and a representative in France.

Forbes keeps
you ahead
in the swim.

Forbes
Capitalist Tool®

TIME

Cablevision
1982

Directors: Seymour Chwast
Alan Peckolick

Representatives: Phyllis Rich Flood
Ilse Lebrecht

U.K.: Pocknell Pushpin Peckolick
Director: David Pocknell
Tel. 07-876-1207

Paris: Evelyne Menasce
Tel. 011-227-2482

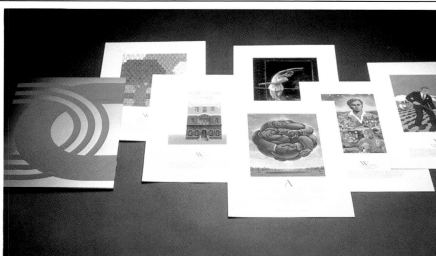

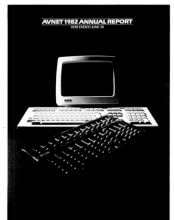

1216 Hawthorne
Houston, Texas 77006
(713) 526-1250

*H*ERRING DESIGN, FOUNDED IN 1973, is a four person design studio specializing in the design and production of brochures, annual reports, editorial design and trademarks for the corporate, hotel, real estate and banking client.

Recent projects have included Home Sports Entertainment (Cable), The Trement House, The San Luis and The Warwick Post Oak (Hotels), 40 WEST 53RD and 53RD AT THIRD (New York Office Buildings), Boccaccio and Miami City Club (Clubs), Vallen Safety Products and Texas Air Corporation (Annual Reports), March of Dimes and Wetmore & Com-

Areas of Houston have a higher infant mortality rate than South Yemen.

In the past decade, Houston has gathered an impressive list of achievements in business, medicine and the arts. Towering buildings dot the downtown skyline, testifying to the city's growth and vitality. The whole world looks on us as a model.

But Houston has a problem. We have an infant mortality rate 20% higher than the national average, higher than some underdeveloped countries. In fact, infant mortality claims more lives each year than traffic fatalities or homicides. In 1981, 872 babies died before they reached their first birthday. Another 287 were stillborn, countless others were miscarried. Beyond all the statistics, what this means is 17 out of 1000 women who entered a hospital to give birth went home empty-handed. Of the babies that did survive, hundreds are born with serious congenital abnormalities that will shorten their lives or require additional prolonged medical care, therapy or institutionalization.

Houston has the somewhat dubious honor of having the largest public maternity hospital in the United States. Last year, 15,000 babies were born at Jefferson Davis Hospital, 35% of all the births in the city. By 1986, Jefferson Davis' birth rate is expected to reach 24,000. Ninety percent of the newborn infants leave the hospital within 24 hours of birth and never receive essential medical services. Of the infants at very high risk for abnormal growth, mental retardation, cerebral palsy and visual and hearing handicaps, almost half do not return for critical follow-up treatment. More than a third of all pregnant women in Houston receive little or no prenatal care.

The major cause of infant death is the poor condition of the infant at birth, due to very low birth weight. Indeed, more than 70% of all infant deaths in Houston occur in the first 28 days, a result of low birth weight and immature organ development. Houston is a young city. The same factors that contribute to our excellent quality of life also attract a younger population of child-bearing age into our city. Almost one-third of all Houston area pregnancies are to teenage mothers, a rate higher than the national average. And teens have a higher incidence of pregnancy related complications than the 20-29 age group, twice as high. Babies born to teenagers are twice as likely to be premature, twice as likely to be low birth weight.

Many may feel these statistics, disturbing as they are, are simply a fact of life. However, enough medical knowledge is currently available to virtually eliminate infant deaths from our society. Many causes of infant mortality have been identified: genetic, biological, environmental, cultural and social. The majority are preventable given the time and money. However, it is a curious commentary on the United States that we spend millions of dollars each year on medical research projects benefitting individuals with an average life expectancy of an additional 5-10 years. Meanwhile, relatively little money is spent on projects that would have a positive impact on the health and well-being of children who have 70 years to live and be productive.

pany (Brochures). The work of Herring Design has been the subject of feature articles in *Communication Arts* Magazine, *Idea* Magazine (Japan), *The Kansas City Star* and the *Houston Post*.

"Design is problem solving. I assume that I can make an image that is attractive. So when sitting down with my clients, the focus is on what they need, what they want to accomplish. The image, whether emotionally compelling or dignified, amusing or serious, comes from the solution to the clients' communication or marketing problem. And we keep in mind that our product must be appropriate to the taste and style of our clients. That the words and images work well together. And that the budget is approached and honored in a businesslike fashion.

That is our theory for doing business. It has enabled us to do some very good work for some very nice clients."

—Jerry Herring

"Every time Tony improves the pizza we change menus in 78 different locations. You talk about a mess."

ROBERT WAGES

Graphic Design
1584 Sheridan Road N.E.
Atlanta, Georgia 30324
(404) 634-1383

*I*N A RENOVATED COW BARN JUST
on the edge of Atlanta's city's
limits, Bob Wages and his design
team create some of the most
distinctive corporate identities
coming out of the South.

Bob's design solutions have proven
effective in fields as diverse as consumer goods, high-tech computer
components, professional sports
and telecommunications.

He enjoys the challenges of packaging assignments and corporate
literature, and specializes in estab-
lishing and implementing graphic
standards for his corporate clients.

1

2

3

4

14

13

12

5

6

7

8

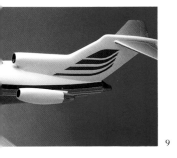

9

10

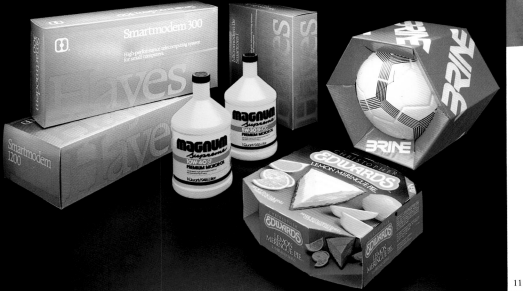

11

One Zoe Street
San Francisco, California 94107
(415) 543-6745

Michael Patrick Cronan DESIGN is engaged in all forms of corporate communication, graphic, exhibit and packaging design. If they have a speciality, it is producing innovative, engaging overall programs. Included here is work for the San Francisco Symphony and their current performance season.

The office works with clients who share the belief that good design is good business. Their client list includes Levi Strauss & Company, Shaklee Corporation, Apple Computer, The Oakland Museum, Mills Memorial Hospital, Children's Hospital of San Francisco, Consolidated Capital Communications Group, Chevron Chemical Company, World Savings and Loan Association, Chronicle Books, Creative Arts Book Company.

BEETHOVEN FESTIVAL

San Francisco Symphony

Edo de Waart, Music Director

June 19–
July 3

Beethoven lives, and San Francisco will be alive with his music this summer.

JIM COTTON GRAPHIC COMMUNICATIONS

13 West 36 Street
New York, N.Y. 10018
212-563-3022

*J*IM COTTON GRAPHIC COMMUNICATIONS specializes in corporate communications, identity systems and marketing. The firm uses the team concept of designer and production specialist to assure design integrity, cost-conscious production and maximum marketing impact.

"My 9 years of experience in the advertising industry gives us a strong marketing awareness," says Jim Cotton, the firm's president. "Our awards are sales results." Jim Cotton's advertising experience was with Benton and Bowles, Grey and Ogilvy & Mather. Accounts included General Electric, Mercedes-

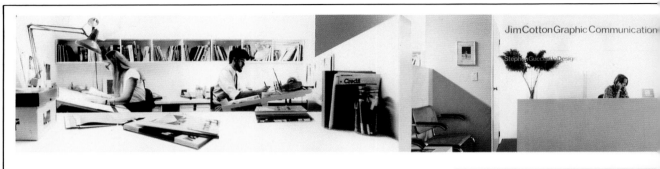

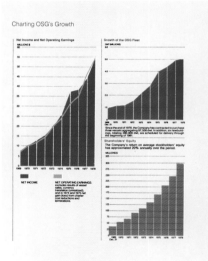

Warner-Amex's preeminence in advanced technology is accentuated in our packaging of their promotional and capabilities documents. Shown here is a proposal summary where we utilized the cover to convey their lead in interactive cable systems.

Clear, concise and attractive charts are a key ingredient in the annual report's ability to communicate the corporate picture to shareholders and the investment community.

We have been responsible for Trafalgar's identity and promotional materials since inception, contributing to their success as a marketer of men's and women's accessories. Shown here is a catalog cover, the Trafalgar trademark and Victory toilet accessories.

The award-winning trademark design shown at right was recently completed as the cornerstone of Tribune's redesigned corporate identity program. Its design dynamics say at once technology and growth.

Benz, Cunard Lines, Crest, Gaines, Canada Dry and Cutty Sark. Special services include: Corporate identity systems, corporate publications, book and periodical design, package design, exhibit design, audio-visual presentations, point-of-sale, direct mail and advertising campaigns.

The client list includes: Equitable Life, Western Electric, Control Data/BTSI, Group W, Warner Amex, Moody's, U.S.T.A., Columbia University, Tribune Cable, French American Group, Trafalgar, Ltd., Four Seasons Hotels, Palmas del Mar Resort, The Westbury Hotel and Travac Charters.

With the aid of our strong graphic treatment, Tribune, a young, aggressive company, has won nearly every franchise they have sought. Shown above is a presentation set, used in a winning effort in partnership with United Cable, carrying our logo/trademark design.

In order to create the excitement and urgency necessary for the Columbia School of Business' Alumni Day Program, our design symbolizes the challenging obstacles in the business world today.

In recognition of the inconsistency and poor readability of their products, brochures, and annuals, Moody's commissioned us to update the complete product line, an example of which is the Reports cover, shown.

Edward Green, Ltd. needed an image of utmost quality and tradition upon entering the U.S. market. Our trademark solution, shown, is an adaptation of Old English trade signs.

415 North Dearborn
Chicago, Illinois 60610
(312) 527-0870

*D*IN & ASSOCIATES PROVIDES planning, development, design and implementation of a broad range of communication projects spanning the disciplines of marketing, advertising, public relations and design:

Corporate Identity Development
  Research, name generation, visual identity and signature development, stationary and forms systems, architectural signage and vehicle identification;
Corporate and Financial Communications
  Financial reports, capabilities brochures, employee communications, recruitment communications and public relations;
Marketing Communications
  Research, communications planning, advertising, product literature, media analysis, planning, purchasing and trafficking, exhibits and trade shows, product packaging, audio-visual presentations

Partial client list:
Aluminum Company of America
Baxter Travenol Laboratories, Inc.
Borg-Warner Corporation
Brunswick Corporation
Fansteel VR/Wesson
Hewitt Associates
Johnson Controls, Inc.
Metropolitan Structures
Motorola, Inc.
Noddings Calamos and Associates
The Quaker Oats Company

Striking. But what does it mean?

Designers can sometimes think in a language of color, style, typography and imagery. A language which speaks to the craft and the art, but not to the intent of design. For as beautiful as any design may be, if it fails to communicate . . . it fails.

Din & Associates plans and participates in the development of *communications*. Our firm is built with professionals from the disciplines of design, public relations and advertising; each contributing synergistically to the goals of reaching and motivating client audiences.

Our designers have collaborated with corporate and marketing communication staffs of organizations that include *Baxter Travenol, Borg-Warner, Brunswick, Hewitt Associates, Johnson Controls, Motorola, Quaker Oats,* and many others. In other situations, Din & Associates has drawn from each of its resources and provided comprehensive, results-oriented plans for these and other clients. In every case however, our award-winning creativity is directed toward helping people gain better understanding of our clients through the use of appropriate communications.

Din & Associates has been recognized for its ability to communicate with employee, investor, technical and customer audiences by identifying the visual and verbal messages that mean the most to them. After all, as the calligraphy clearly states, ''each group speaks its own language.''

If effective, appropriate and meaningful communications are important, consider Din & Associates. Contact Janet Zaleski, at 312.527.0870. She will be pleased to discuss how our business can help people understand your business better.

Din & Associates

Business Marketing and Communications
Chicago, Illinois
312.527.0870

HINKLE, CRAWFORD, DAVIES, INC.
Creative Services

1440 Terrace Drive
Tulsa, Oklahoma 74104
(918) 744-1101

*H*INKLE, CRAWFORD, DAVIES, Inc. has been solving marketing problems through design for 32 years. The firm specializes in:
Corporate Identity
Corporate Communications
Annual Reports
Architectural Signage
Environmental Graphics
Packaging
Product and Sales Promotion

Clients include:
Applied Automation, Inc.
American Beauty Products
Blue Cross and Blue Shield of
 Oklahoma
Carapace, Inc.
C-E Invalco
Oil and Gas Journal
Phillips Chemical Company
Phillips Petroleum Company
QuikTrip Corporation
Sunbeam Leisure Products
 Company
Telex Computer Products, Inc.
Toshiba International Corporation
Tulsa Opera, Inc.
United States Department of
 Energy
Webbcraft, Inc.
Zebco

Identities shown at far right, clockwise:
 Tulsa Opera; Sober, Logsdon, Woody, Interior Design/Space Planning; Silverstone Apartments; Cotton-Banks, Information Systems.

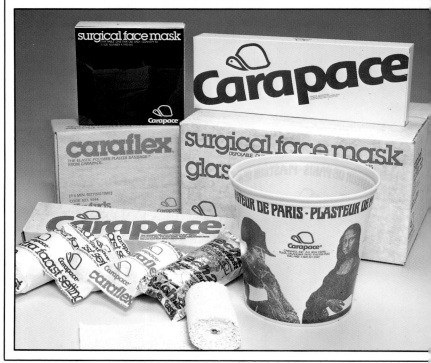

271 Madison Avenue
New York, N.Y. 10016
(212) 683-6592

*O*NE WORD SUMS UP
Modi & Beckler Design:
Integrity.

M&B offers creative
design solutions.
Because they investigate
every aspect of a product.
And take pains to under-
stand a client's goals.

Their design is strong.
The message clear.
And challenging clients
commend their work.

For theirs is not the
standard approach.
But highly personalized,
arresting design.
Unique answers to
unique needs.

M&B won't just take
any assignment.
You can't further a
client's goals if you
don't believe in them.

*Rohit Modi and Shelley
Beckler with New York City
Mayor Edward Koch at special
ceremony commending their
poster design.*

1) Symbol: Frank Spencer
Heart Research Foundation.
2) Symbol: Mental Retardation.
3) Logotype: The Learning Child.
4) Symbol: Gujarat State
Fertilizer Corporation.
5) Symbol: Ashoka Hotels.
6) Trademark: Volunteer Lawyers
for the Arts.
7) Symbol: Institute for
the Advancement of Health.
8) Trademark: The Design
Collaborative.
9) Trademark: Advertising
Artists Association.

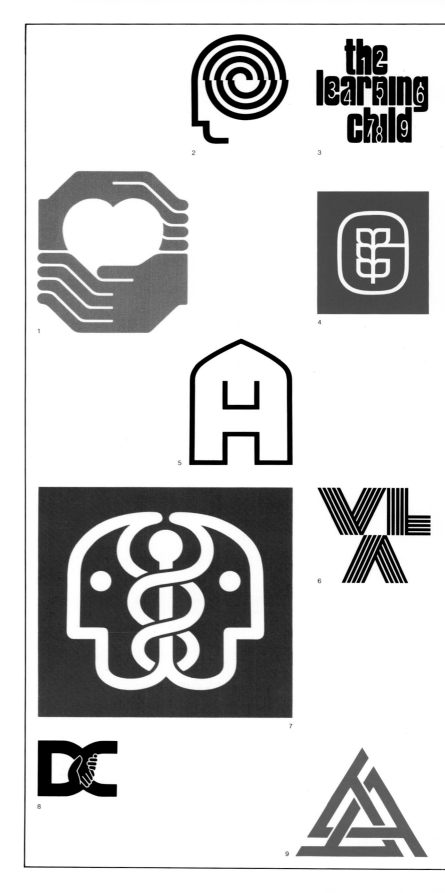

11

10

12

14

13

10) Book Design: Volunteer
Lawyers for the Arts.
11) Packaging: Nature
Fresh, Inc.
12-13) Corporate Identity:
Katzman Oring Associates
and DAK Excess Limited.
14) Exhibition: Planned
Parenthood of NYC.
15) Poster: Unicef.

15

1604 Vista Del Mar Avenue
Los Angeles, CA 90028
(213) 467-4681

WHITE + ASSOCIATES IS A graphics communications firm, specializing in new product introductions and the revitalization and repositioning of existing products. Their design approach is in sync with marketing strategy to provide creative, attractive, and sound solutions. The projects shown reflect their strength at solving marketing problems.

"I am impressed with the degree of creative involvement shown in the need analysis and proposals . . . and with the unusual degree of documentation they provide . . . This was invaluable . . ."

Clifford Silver, Director
MAI/Basic Four Information
Systems

"Always looking for new ways to meet traditional marketing needs . . . met all of our deadlines . . . [They] deliver top quality in everything they do . . . it's one of the best creative shops I ever worked with . . ."

Alan H. Lewis,
Director of Marketing
Knudsen Corporation

". . . provided highly creative solutions and operated under tight cost constraints and schedule demands . . ."

John Kempton, Manager
Jet Propulsion Laboratory

". . . were able to absorb an enormous amount of input in a short time and provide a solution that has successfully launched this product line . . ."

Michael R. Robarts,
Advertising Mgr.
Eldon Office Products

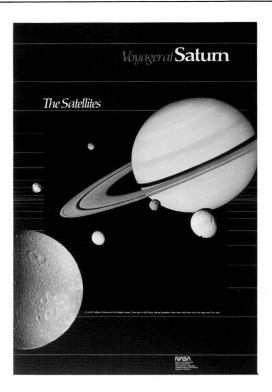

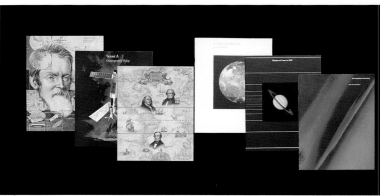

NASA/JPL

Problem: To educate and inform the public about planetary exploration programs at NASA/JPL.

Solution: Created memorable images for diverse audiences by providing unique design concepts for photographs and data. Widely distributed to universities, major NASA contractors, observatories, museums, Congressional committees, etc.

Results: World-wide recognition of and response to NASA/JPL's programs.

ELDON OFFICE PRODUCTS

Problem: New product line entry into the computer supplies market needed brand mark and package development.

Solution: Developed package and mark with high shelf impact. The design promotes the versatility and high tech look of the product.

Results: One of Eldon's most successful product launches. Mediabank immediately went into back order.

KNUDSEN CORPORATION
(Dairy Products)

Problem: To enter the personal care product category by creating a brand personality and product benefit story for Milk Maid.

Solution: Development of all test-market materials, including the design and construction of on-site sales kiosk.

Results: Personal care industry leaders recognized Knudsen's aggressive efforts as the product was very successful under test-market conditions.

MAI/BASIC FOUR BUSINESS PRODUCTS
(Computer Hardware)

Problem: To create a merchandising center for the sell-in of the S/10 microcomputer. Objectives: to demonstrate marketability of P.O.P., to educate the customer, to sell the product.

Solution: Retail and trade show displayer and merchandising materials. Innovative use of modules affords both customer benefits and assembly ease. Bold graphics produce a strong visual identity.

Results: The displayer and materials represented a key element of the launch that was well-received by prospective dealers.

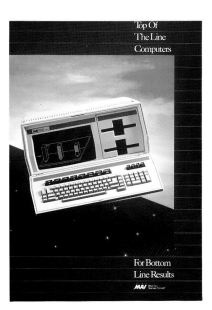

TRIBICH DESIGN ASSOCIATES, INC.

150 East 35th Street
New York, NY 10016
(212) 679-6016

"Maybe we could say we offer each job?"

"You can't lie in an ad."

"Well we're a full-service design firm."

"That's true. And hundreds of others describe themselves the same way. We want to say something different."

"We are different. That's no lie."

Norstar Bancorp

"Yes, but how do we . . ."

"We do lots of things, for all kinds of companies."

"Maybe we should . . ."

". . . Brochures, annuals packaging, promotion, I.D., logos, ads. Hm, that's —"

"And our clients like us I mean, 80% of our work is repeat business."

Academy Broadway
Albany Academy
American Express
Association of
  Junior Leagues
Athlone Industries
Beneficial
Beth Abraham Hospital
Brooklyn Hospital
Citicorp
Citicorp Services
Comstock
Doctor's Hospital
Doespun
Dugan & Meyers
General Aviation
  Manufacturers Assoc.
General Signal
F.B. Hall & Co.
Harcourt Brace
  Jovanovich
H.J. Heinz
Hospital for
  Special Surgery
Huber Hunt and Nichols
Iroquois Brands
Kurzweil Computer
  Products
Lake Placid Winter
  Olympic Committee
Manufacturers
  Hanover Trust
Mickelberry
Mt. Sinai Medical Center
National Telephone
  Planning
Norstar Bancorp
Ogden
Paine Webber
T.J. Ross & Company
Science Management
SCM
Sony
Sperry & Hutchinson
Sportsotron
Standard & Poor's
Tecton Media
Torcon
Tosco
United Bank New York

a free Swedish massage with

"We're growing. 300% in the last three years. That says something."

"They _do_ like us. Remember the Jay Tribich look-alike contest?"

(laughter)

"After three years of seeing Jay's cardigan sweaters, we walked in one day and everybody at Norstar, even top management, had one on."

(laughter)

"We always deliver on time. Remember when we were on our way to deliver the comps on that Sony project, at 2 A.M., to meet that impossible—"

Sony

"... That deadline. And the driver's door opened while he was turning a corner and he nearly fell out of the cab."

"And there we were in the back seat, looking at each other, and you said . . ."

"I said 'Protect those comps'."

(laughter)

Athlone Industries

"Maybe sincerity. We take our work to heart. All of us are . . ."

"We always come through. Creatively, and . . . you know . . . within the budget, on time . . ."

"And that's important."

"O.K. But how do we say all that in an ad?"

(pause)

"I still like the Swedish massage idea."

(212) 679-6016.
Or write for our brochure.

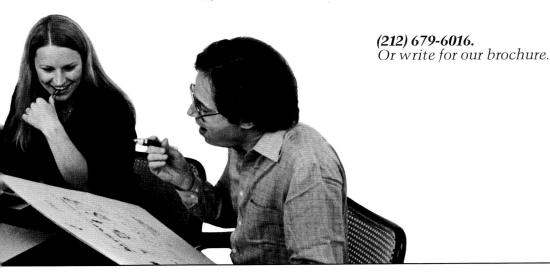

Suite 3607
233 East Wacker Drive
Chicago, Illinois 60601
(312) 565-1114

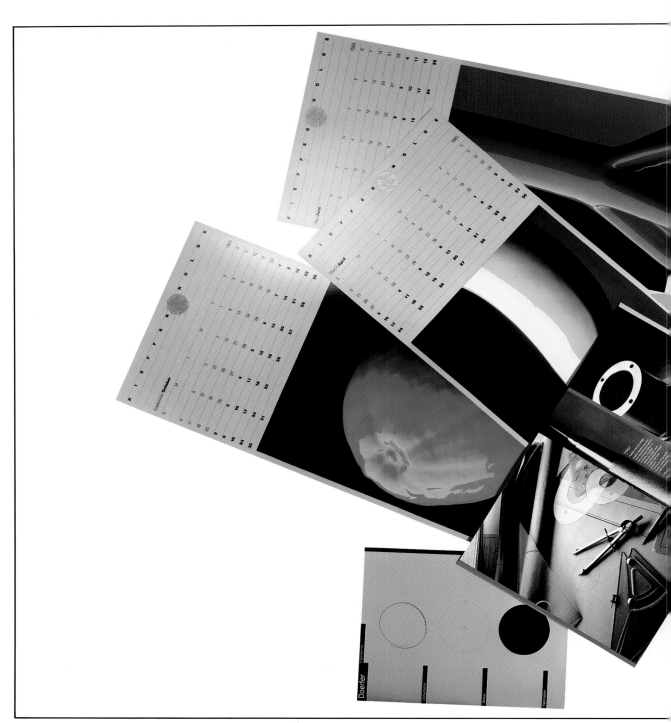

VANDERBYL DESIGN

One Zoe Street
San Francisco, California 94107
(415) 543-8447

Trademarks
1. *Yachtmen's Exchange*
2. *Community Action Team
   of Foremost McKesson*
3. *Napa Valley Corporate Park*
4. *California Conservation Corps*
5. *Met One*
6. *Canyon Lakes*
7. *Marina Bay*
8. *The Court*

Mindset Computers
9. *Institutional Poster*

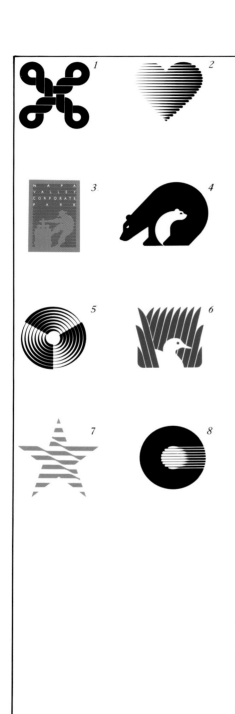

PLUMB DESIGN GROUP INC.

57 East 11th Street
New York, N.Y. 10003
(212) 673-3490

*T*HE PRODUCT COMES FIRST. BE IT a thing or a service, the product alone is the company's raison d'etre.

Design is what defines the product—functionally, visually, and ergonomically.

And, because producer and product are one and the same, design defines the producer as well.

Product, corporate image, communications, working environment, packaging, promotional material—

Each is part of the whole. The function, appearance, and perception of each affects the quality of all the others.

The goal is a harmonious, integrated whole. The means lie in the hands of the designer.

Plumb Design Group—generalists who know how to conceive of the whole. Specialists in the skills needed to bring together each of its parts.

Plumb Design Group—experts in the successful development of interrelated corporate design programs.

Plumb Design Group—20 years of experience with a brand new point of view.

Plumb Design Group—masters of the creative tools that sharpen your competitive edge.

Plumb Design Group—the means to achieving your corporate end.

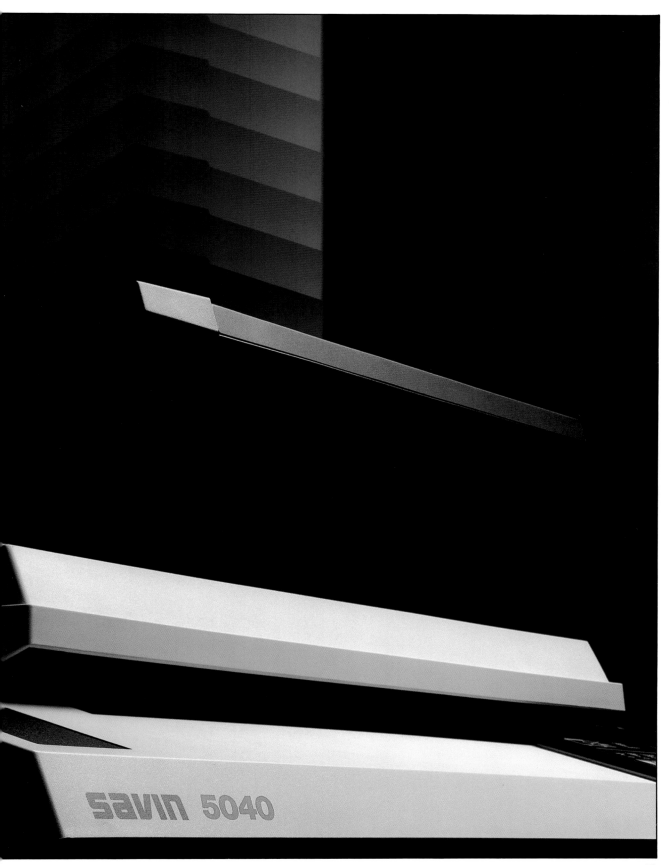

SERGE BEVIL DESIGNS, INC.

156 Fifth Avenue
New York, N.Y. 10010
(212) 242-1900

*D*ESIGN + CONSULTING
in Promotional and Corporate
Communications.

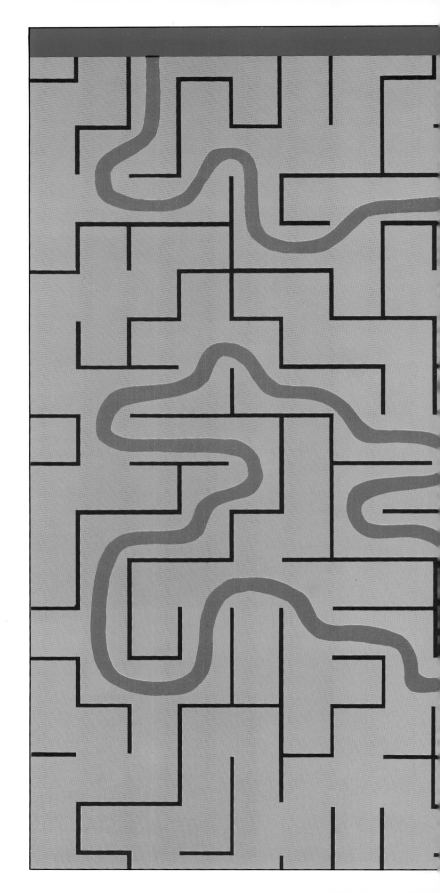

Have your creative goals led you in this direction?

We at Serge Bevil Designs clearly understand the importance of pinpointing your objectives to avoid the frustration of costly runarounds.

We are an established design firm that focuses on successfully promoting our clients' products, services, and identities through a variety of marketing and creative media.

CORPORATE COMMUNICATIONS
LOGO DESIGN / IDENTITY SYSTEMS / SIGNAGE / ANNUAL REPORTS

ADVERTISING
COPY / CAMPAIGNS / PLACEMENT

COLLATERAL
DIRECT MAIL / SALES PROMOTION / POSTERS / BILLBOARDS

PUBLICATION DESIGN
CONSUMER AND TRADE MAGAZINES / BOOKS / COVERS / MASTHEADS

VISUAL PRESENTATIONS
SCRIPTS / DESIGN / PHOTOGRAPHY / POST-PRODUCTION

PACKAGING
CONFIGURATIONS / GRAPHICS / BRAND AND PRODUCT DEVELOPMENT

Our goals are precise:
To generate tangible results by selecting appropriate visual presentations of sound marketing directions. To define, or to redefine the problems each project presents. Because often to identify a problem is to delineate a successful solution.

Our methods, effective.
We isolate solid concepts based on accurate information about your particular product or service. But concepts are only a beginning—ideas must be made visible: and through our experience, knowledge, and resources, we can make our ideas work for you. Practically, Economically. Nevertheless, memorably.

To see how we've brought our principles to bear on past projects, give us a call: we'd like to show you our work personally and discuss your communicative goals.

Serge Bevil Designs, Inc.
156 Fifth Ave., N.Y.C., N.Y. 10010
(212) 242-1900

HARRY MURPHY + FRIENDS

225 Miller Avenue
Mill Valley, CA 94941
(415) 383-8586

*S*INCE 1966 HARRY MURPHY + FRIENDS has produced successful identity and communication materials for hundreds of corporations.
Harry Murphy + Friends has won more than 800 national and international design awards.

CORPORATE IDENTITY

1. Steaks Unique
   Steak house restaurant chain.
2. Pool Sweep
   Pool cleaning equipment.
3. Jack Klassen
   Building contractor.
4. U.S. Team
   Men's sportswear line.
5. Carmel Plaza
   Shopping center.
6. Logo Stores
   Name brand fashions.
7. Jim Fisher & Associates
   Real estate management.
8. Anneberg Gallery
   Art and craft gallery.
9. Harbor Bay
   Business park development.
10. Jamboree Stores
    Children's clothing store chain.
11. Marin Swim School
    Swimming instruction program.
12. Z's Buffet
    Buffet-style restaurant chain.
13. The Gap Stores
    Annual Report for casual clothing chain.
14. Vidiom Stores
    Video products store chain.
15. St. George Spirits
    Packaging for fruit brandies.
16. Thomson CSF Broadcast
    Exhibition for manufacturer of color television cameras.
17. The Small Things Company
    Packaging for pot pourri.
18. Ted's
    Cocktail lounge.

1.

7.

2.

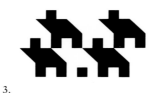

8.

3.

9.

4.

10.

5.

11.

6.

12.

13.

16.

14.

17.

15.

18.

PRINCIPALS INDEX

INDEX

CLIENT INDEX

ON THE GUILD

*T*he Graphic Artists Guild was founded 15 years ago by a dozen professional illustrators in the Detroit area to affect industry standards and practices. Today the Guild has a membership of 5,000 artists in every professional discipline, with regional chapters in New York, Atlanta, Baltimore, Boston, Buffalo, Indianapolis and Burlington, Vermont.

Each chapter meets frequently to develop and run programs for its members, discuss industry issues, establish regional goals, and retain membership contact. The National Board meets monthly to establish national goals, assess programs and projects that affect all members, and to keep board members apprised of regional activities. Twice a year the full National Board, including regional representatives, meets for updates on activities, review of national programs, and to decide on future projects for the Guild. It's this constant communication on local and national levels that keeps the Guild close to its membership and aware of what's happening in the industry. Members within the various disciplines—graphic design, illustration, production graphics, textile and related design fields—share information, discuss problems and act to improve the profession.

From its inception, the Guild has reached out to other creative professionals and their organizations to form coalitions on issues of mutual concern. The first creators' coalition was formed in 1976 around an issue of copyright control. That coalition has since grown to include 42 creators' organizations that represent illustrators, photographers, journalists and freelance writers, among others. In the past three years the coalition has been actively lobbying for an amendment to the 1976 copyright law that will eliminate situations in which work-for-hire can be used. This is the first time that creators from the graphic arts have joined together on a legislative issue.

The work-for-hire provision allows a client, in certain specified instances, to become the creator of the work. Through work-for-hire a client may, in these cases, buy a piece of art, claim authorship, alter or reuse it in any way without the approval of the original creator of the work. As Guild members reported an increasing number of such incidents, the Guild's lobbying efforts accelerated. In October, 1982, the U.S. Senate, urged by the Graphic Artists Guild, held a hearing on the issue. As a result, legislation to amend the work-for-hire provision is expected to be introduced in Congress in the near future.

On a state level, the Guild began working in New York and California on the Moral Rights and Fair Practices bills. Moral Rights allows an artist legal recourse when a creative work has been defaced, altered or mutilated by a client to the detriment of the creator's reputation or work. The act also allows creators to claim or disclaim authorship for the work in those instances. A version of this law was passed in California in 1982, and the Moral Rights Act was signed into law by New York's Governor Cuomo in August, 1983.

The Fair Practices Act, signed into law in New York in 1983, was the result of four years of lobbying by the Guild. It provides that the original artwork remains the property of the artist unless it is specifically sold in writing. Further, any ambiguity in the language of a contract results in the presumption of ownership rights remaining with the artist. Since most graphic artists make at least part of their livelihood on the resale of reproduction rights and additionally, by the sale of the original art, this law is critical to the economic survival of these artists.

Representatives of the Guild went to Washington in 1979 to give an in-depth presentation on graphic design to the Copyright Office. They presented an extensive visual and verbal analysis that showed how most graphic design is a form of creative expression worthy of copyright protection. As a result, the Copyright Office reassessed its interpretation of graphic design for the purposes of copyright law. Graphic designers are now vested with the same status that is applied to illustrators, photographers and fine artists.

The Graphic Artists Guild brings a wide variety of artists together to work on contractual standards, pricing and artists rights legislation. It enables members to communicate with their professional peers and allows each to take advantage of the group's experiences.

Membership benefits include the Guild's lobbying efforts on state and federal levels, publications on business standards and practices, pricing guidelines, educational seminars and workshops, and group health, life and disability plans.

The Guild offers an educational program, available to members and non-members alike, which includes business schools in each regional chapter. Seminars and workshops are held on subjects such as negotiating, self-promotion techniques, running a business, new technologies and other business-related issues. Additionally, the Guild publishes model contracts and forms, and books on pricing and ethical issues.

*M*ost rewarding for Guild members is their activity on a more philosophical level. Together, they work to cultivate the *respect, support* and *dignity* that all artists deserve as professionals. And as professionals, members of the Guild understand their responsibilities to promote the highest level of professionalism in their industry.

The Guild is totally egalitarian. Its constitution states that it will accept any working professional graphic artist as a voting member, "regardless of race, gender or belief." It attracts the most gifted artists, since they are the ones who recognize most readily the need to protect their professional integrity and their art.

This volume of Directory 4, the Corporate & Communications Design Annual, is the first of its kind ever compiled and published. We believe that the work on these pages presents some of the best examples in contemporary design from across the nation. And, we think you'll agree that the work here represents the diversity and excitement in the profession today.

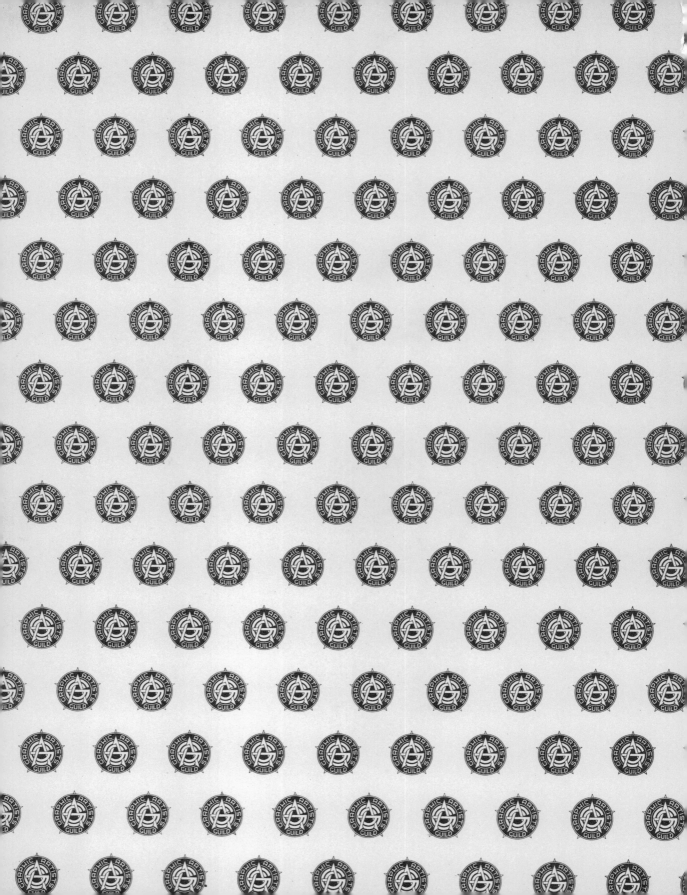